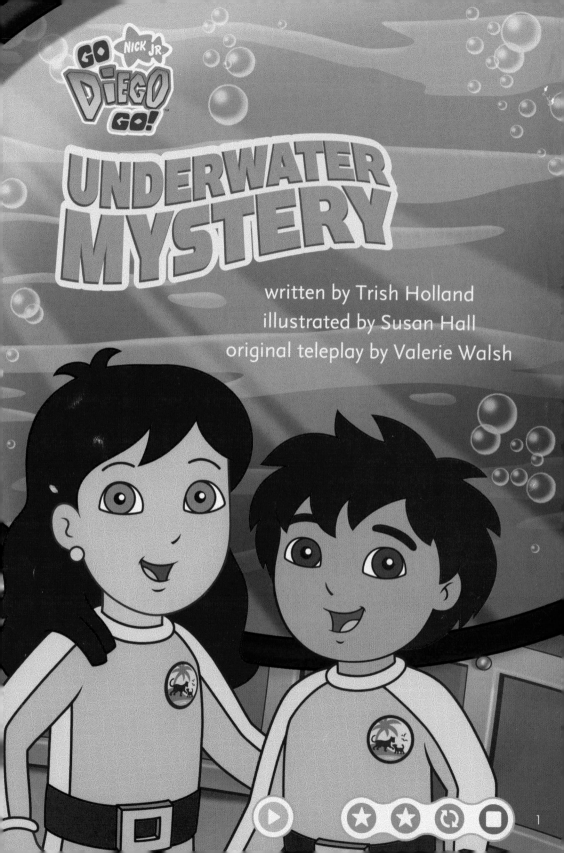

UNDERWATER MYSTERY

written by Trish Holland
illustrated by Susan Hall
original teleplay by Valerie Walsh

"¡*Hola!*" says Diego. "I'm Diego and this is my sister, Alicia. We're Animal Scientists."

"Today we're exploring the ocean, looking for new animals," says Alicia.

Suddenly, they hear, "Help! Help!"

"That sounds like an animal in trouble! We've got to help!" says Diego.

Diego and Alicia swim quickly to the Rescue Submarine.

Click the camera shows them the picture of a very big fish. The fish is in cold ocean water. She is bumping into icebergs.

"It's a mystery fish!" says Click.

"*¡Al rescate!* To the rescue!" say Diego and Alicia.

They take the Rescue Submarine into the cold ocean water.

"There she is!" shouts Diego. "*Hola*, fish. We're Animal Rescuers. I'm Diego and this is my sister, Alicia. What's your name?"

"My name is Lucy," says the fish. "I'm lost and cold."

"We'll help you find your home," says Diego. "What kind of fish are you?"

"I don't know," Lucy says.

SANTA MARIA URBAN MINISTRY
OF SAN JOSE
778 SOUTH ALMADEN AVE.
SAN JOSE, CA 95110
(408) 292-3314

7

To take Lucy home, Diego and Alicia need to find out what kind of fish Lucy is. They have three clues:

1. Lucy is a very big fish.
2. She has spots and stripes.
3. She swims slowly, and wiggles her tail from side to side.

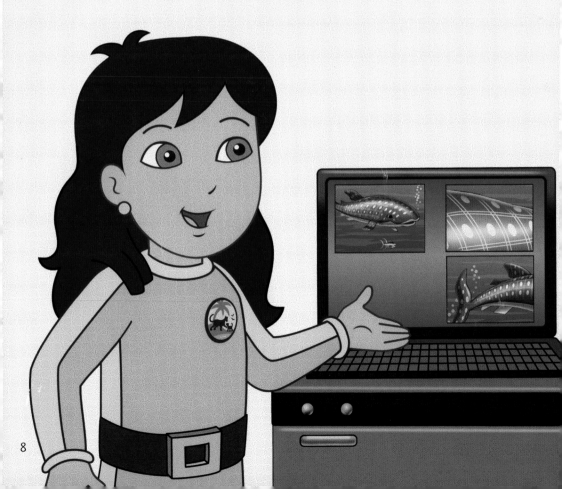

"We've got to find more clues," says Diego.

Diego looks at the thermometer.

"It's too cold for you here," says Diego.
"We'll take you to warmer water."

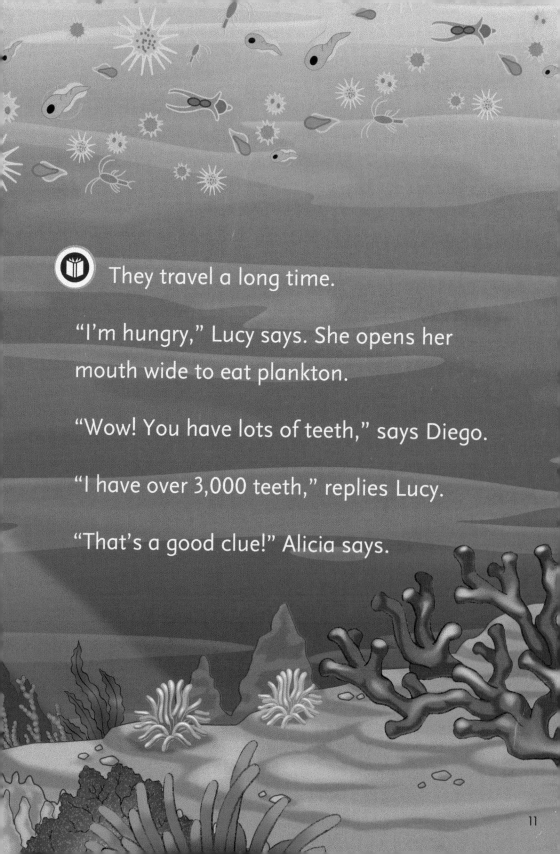

They travel a long time.

"I'm hungry," Lucy says. She opens her mouth wide to eat plankton.

"Wow! You have lots of teeth," says Diego.

"I have over 3,000 teeth," replies Lucy.

"That's a good clue!" Alicia says.

They continue
their journey.
Lucy swims beside
the Rescue Submarine.

"I can't wait to find out what
kind of fish I am!" she says.

Suddenly, they see a
hammerhead shark.
He is caught in a net.
"Oh, I can save him,"
cries Lucy.

Lucy uses her large head to lift the net.
The shark swims out.

"Look, Diego. Lucy has a fin on her back
just like that little hammerhead shark.
Maybe Lucy is a shark, too," says Alicia.

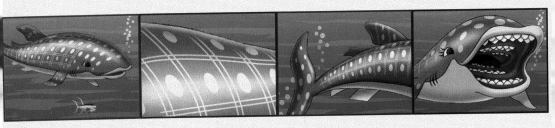

Alicia and Diego have five clues now.
They ask the computer what kind of shark
Lucy is. An answer flashes onto the screen.

"Lucy, you're a whale shark!" says Diego.

"You're the biggest fish in the ocean," says Alicia.

"Yippeeeeee!" shouts Lucy. "I love being a whale shark!"

"Whale sharks live in warm water. The water here is warm. Lucy, you're home!" says Diego.

"Now we can look for your friends," Alicia says.

SANTA MARIA URBAN MINISTRY
OF SAN JOSE
778 SOUTH ALMADEN AVE.
SAN JOSE, CA 95110
(408) 292-3314

"I see them! There are my friends! Thank you for rescuing me Diego and Alicia!" Lucy says.

"*De nada*, Lucy," say Diego and Alicia. "*¡Hasta luego!*"

The End

lip

hip

cap

tap

l
t
h
s

c
n
t
m

ip

ap

Say Click! Take A Pic!

tip

sip

nap

map

trumpet

rock

sun

sword

sea

parrot

rockfish   swordfish

parrotfish   sunfish

seaweed   seahorse

trumpetfish   seashell

fish

weed

shell

horse

Deep Sea Discovery

Sea Animal Exploration

crab

jellyfish

sea star

pelican

albatross

sandpiper

angelfish

parrotfish

yellowfin tuna

stingray

whale shark

hammerhead shark

D0959230

SANTA MARIA URBAN MINISTRY
OF SAN JOSE
778 SOUTH B___

Let's Play Tag!

 Read the Page

▶ Read the Story

↻ Repeat

■ Stop

★ Game

★ Level 1 ★★ Level 2 ★★★ Level 3

TO USE THIS BOOK WITH THE TAG™ READER you must download audio from the LeapFrog Connect application.
The LeapFrog Connect application can be installed from the CD provided with your Tag Reader or at leapfrog.com/tag.